Life Cycles

Painted Lady Butterflies

by Donna Schaffer

Consultant:
Phil Schappert, Ph.D.
The Lepidopterists' Society,
Department of Zoology,
University of Texas

Bridgestone Books
an imprint of Capstone Press
Mankato, Minnesota

Bridgestone Books are published by Capstone Press
151 Good Counsel Drive, P.O. Box 669, Mankato, Minnesota 56002
http://www.capstone-press.com

Library of Congress Cataloging-in-Publication Data
Schaffer, Donna.
    Painted lady butterflies/by Donna Schaffer.
    p. cm.—(Life cycles)
    Includes bibliographical references (p. 23) and index.
    Summary: Describes the physical characteristics, habits, and stages of development
of painted lady butterflies.
    ISBN 0-7368-0211-8
    1. Painted lady (Insect)—Life cycles—Juvenile literature. [1. Painted lady (Insect)
2. Butterflies.] I. Title. II. Series: Schaffer, Donna. Life cycles.
QL561.N9S36   1999
595.78'9—dc21

98-53026
CIP
AC

Editorial Credits
Christy Steele, editor; Steve Weil/Tandem Design, cover designer; Linda Clavel,
    illustrator; Kimberly Danger, photo researcher

Photo Credits
Charles W. Melton, 4
Connie Toops, 8-9
David Liebman, 12, 14, 18
Fred Siskind, 10, 16, 20, 20 (inset)
KAC Productions/John & Gloria Tueten, cover
Rob and Ann Simpson, 6

2 3 4 5 6 04 03 02 01 00

Table of Contents

Life Cycle Diagram 4
The Life Cycle 5
The Painted Lady Butterfly 7
Mating 8
Eggs 11
Caterpillars 13
Molting 15
The Pupa 17
Chrysalis Changes 19
Adult Painted Lady Butterflies 21

Hands On: Make Butterfly Bait 22
Words to Know 23
Read More 23
Useful Addresses 24
Internet Sites 24
Index 24

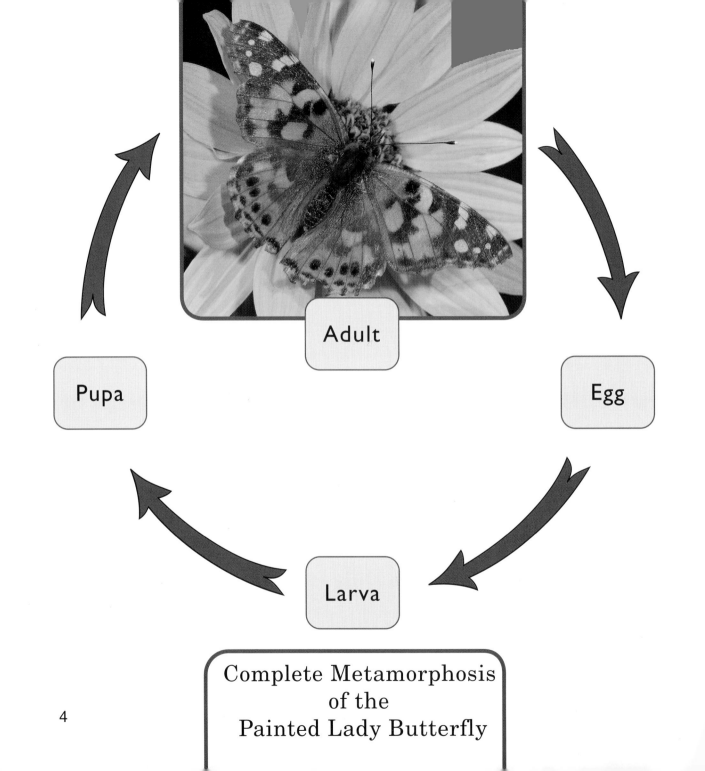

Pupa

Adult

Egg

Larva

Complete Metamorphosis
of the
Painted Lady Butterfly

4

The Life Cycle

The painted lady butterfly goes through complete metamorphosis. Four stages happen during complete metamorphosis. A painted lady butterfly's body changes its form four times.

The first stage is the egg. Painted lady butterflies grow in eggs during this stage. They are caterpillars when they hatch. Caterpillars are the second, or larval, stage. Larvas become chrysalises during the pupal stage. The caterpillar changes and grows adult body parts during this third stage. Finally, the chrysalis becomes an adult butterfly.

These stages make up the painted lady butterfly's life cycle. Living things go through cycles of birth, growth, reproduction, and death. Painted lady butterflies are born when they hatch from eggs. They eat and grow during the larval stage. They become adults during the pupal stage. They reproduce during the adult stage. Finally, painted lady butterflies die after laying eggs.

The Painted Lady Butterfly

The painted lady butterfly is one of more than 20,000 butterfly species. Each species has its own color patterns and features. *Vanessa cardui* is the scientific name for painted lady butterflies.

Painted lady butterflies are dark brown. They have orange, yellow, and white spots on their wings. They are about 3 inches (8 centimeters) wide across their open wings.

Painted lady butterflies live on every continent except Australia and Antarctica. They live in open areas such as fields and meadows.

Painted lady butterflies are insects. Like all insects, they have six jointed legs and three body sections. These sections are the head, thorax, and abdomen. The eyes and antennas are on the head. The wings and legs attach to the thorax. The stomach is in the abdomen.

● ● ● ● **The painted lady butterfly's nickname is the Cosmopolitan. It lives in more areas of the world than any other butterfly.**

Mating

Adult painted lady butterflies are in the final life stage. During this stage, they mate and produce young. But they first must find mates.

Males search for females in two ways. Some males patrol for females. These males fly around a large area to search for females.

Other males pick a territory. They drive out any males who come into their territories. Some males wait on rocks, plants, or trees in their territories. They follow any female that flies past them. Males and females mate after they find each other.

Some male painted lady butterflies wait in their territories until females fly past them.

Eggs

The female painted lady butterfly searches for food plants such as thistles, soybeans, or mallow. She lays eggs on the undersides of leaves or in other hidden places. This helps protect the eggs from enemies. The female also leaves a scent that warns other butterflies to stay away from the eggs.

Females lay green-blue eggs. Adult females lay eggs in spring and summer in the northern United States and Canada. Females lay eggs all year long in the southern United States.

The egg is the first stage in a painted lady butterfly's life cycle. A butterfly larva grows inside the egg. The larva hatches after about five days.

A larva also is called a caterpillar. This tiny wormlike creature has strong mandibles. The caterpillar uses these mouthparts to eat its way out of the eggshell.

● ● ● ● **Painted lady butterfly eggs are difficult to see. Each egg is about the size of a pinhead.**

Caterpillars

In their second life stage, painted lady butterflies are caterpillars. This stage lasts about two weeks.

Caterpillars breathe through spiracles along their abdomens. These round holes let air into and out of the body.

Caterpillars have three pairs of legs on the thorax. These legs have claws to support them as they move from leaf to leaf.

Caterpillars also have five pairs of short, fat prolegs along the abdomen. These legs help caterpillars grip leaves while they eat.

A hard outer covering called an exoskeleton protects caterpillars. Animals such as birds, bats, and spiders eat caterpillars. These predators may have a hard time breaking through the exoskeleton.

● ● ● ● Caterpillars spend most of their time eating.

Molting

A caterpillar must shed its exoskeleton to grow. This process is called molting. A caterpillar stops eating when it is ready to molt. The caterpillar makes a nest with a spinneret. This body part near its mouth releases sticky strings that become hard. The nest gives caterpillars a safe place to molt.

The caterpillar releases a liquid that loosens the exoskeleton. The exoskeleton splits. The caterpillar then crawls out of its old covering.

A caterpillar eats and grows. The caterpillar is ready to molt again when the new exoskeleton becomes tight and hard.

Painted lady caterpillars molt five times. The time between each molt is called an instar. After each molt, the caterpillar is in a new instar.

A caterpillar in its final instar is about 1 inch (2.5 centimeters) long. The caterpillar is black with a yellow line down each side of the body.

This caterpillar is inside its nest. It is getting ready to molt.

The Pupa

Caterpillars in their final instar prepare for their next life stage. They stop moving and eating. They use their spinnerets to spin a silk circle.

Caterpillars then hang upside down with their bodies in the shape of a J. They attach themselves to the silk circle with their prolegs. Caterpillars molt for the last time.

After the final molt, caterpillars enter the pupal stage. A pupa also is called a chrysalis. The hard exoskeleton of the chrysalis protects it from enemies. The chrysalis cannot move around as a caterpillar can.

Most painted lady butterflies stay in the pupal stage for about 10 days. Painted lady butterflies may stay in the pupal stage longer. Chrysalises change more quickly in warm weather than cold weather. They may remain in the pupal stage for weeks or months if it is cold.

● ● ● ● **This caterpillar is ready to become a chrysalis.**

Chrysalis Changes

The chrysalis becomes a butterfly during the pupal stage. Four large, scaly wings develop. The prolegs disappear and three pairs of jointed legs grow.

Mouthparts change and a proboscis grows. Butterflies use this tube-shaped tongue to drink nectar from flowers.

Large, compound eyes grow. These eyes will allow the butterfly to see color and to see in all directions. A pair of long antennas develops. Adult butterflies use their antennas like noses to pick up scents.

As the chrysalis changes, the exoskeleton becomes more transparent. The growing butterfly can be seen through the clear covering. The adult breaks out of its exoskeleton after seven to 10 days. The painted lady butterfly is then in its final life stage.

The color of the chrysalis helps it blend in with surrounding plants. This camouflage helps keep the chrysalis safe.

Adult Painted Lady Butterflies

Painted lady butterflies have two pairs of wings. The wings are damp and folded when the butterflies first crawl out of their exoskeletons. But the wings dry out and become hard and strong.

Painted lady butterflies can fly long distances. Sometimes they migrate to find food. They fly to faraway places after storms, floods, and other bad weather.

Butterflies drink nectar from flowers and sap from trees. Butterflies use their antennas to smell nectar. They taste nectar with their feet.

Butterflies also pollinate flowers as they drink nectar. They carry pollen from one flower to another as they fly. Pollination is needed for flowers to reproduce.

Painted lady butterflies live for about two weeks. They use this time to mate and to lay eggs. This process continues the life cycle.

● ● ● ● **Painted lady butterflies crawl out of their old exoskeletons. They dry their wings before flying.**

Hands On: Make Butterfly Bait

Painted lady butterflies smell sweet nectar with their antennas. They use their feet to taste nectar. You can make butterfly bait to attract butterflies.

What You Need

A bowl   A spoon
Sugar   A thick, colored sponge
Water

What You Do

1. Put 5 cups of water in the bowl.
2. Put 1 cup of sugar in the bowl.
3. Stir the water and the sugar together. This is the bait.
4. Pour some of the bait over the sponge. Put the sponge back in the bowl. Make sure the top of the sponge sticks up above the bait.
5. Put the bowl outdoors. Watch for butterflies.

Painted lady butterflies will see the sponge and smell the butterfly bait. They will think the sponge is a flower. You can see how the butterflies use their proboscis to drink.

Words to Know

chrysalis (CHRIS-ah-liss)—the pupal stage of a butterfly
exoskeleton (eks-oh-SKEL-uh-tuhn)—a hard, bony covering on the outside of an animal
instar (IN-star)—a stage between molts in the life cycle of many insects
mandibles (MAN-duh-buhlz)—strong mouthparts used to chew
proboscis (pro-BOSS-kiss)—a tubelike mouthpart used to drink nectar
spinneret (spin-nuh-RET)—a body part used to make silk thread
spiracles (SPEER-uh-kuhlss)—tiny holes through which some insects and spiders breathe

Read More

Hamilton, Kersten. *The Butterfly Book: A Kid's Guide to Attracting, Raising, and Keeping Butterflies.* Santa Fe, N.M.: John Muir Publications, 1997.

Heligmann, Deborah. *From Caterpillar to Butterfly.* New York: HarperCollins, 1996.

Useful Addresses

Butterfly World
P.O. Box 36
Coombs, BC VQR 1MO
Canada

The Lepidopterists' Society
c/o Los Angeles County
Museum of Natural History
900 Exposition Boulevard
Los Angeles, CA 90007-4057

Internet Sites

The Butterfly Web Site
http://mgfx.com/butterfly
The Lepidopterists' Society
http://www.furman.edu/~snyder/snyder/lep

Index

caterpillar, 5, 11, 13, 15, 17
chrysalis, 5, 17, 19
egg, 5, 11, 21
exoskeleton, 13, 15, 21
instar, 15, 17
larva, 5, 11
mandibles, 11
mate, 8, 21

metamorphosis, 5
migrate, 21
molt, 15, 17
proboscis, 19
pupa, 17
spinneret, 15, 17
spiracles, 13
thistles, 11